Who Was
Theodore Roosevelt?

Who Was
Theodore Roosevelt?

By Michael Burgan

Illustrated by Jerry Hoare

Grosset & Dunlap

An Imprint of Penguin Group (USA) LLC

For all the history teachers who have inspired me—MB

GROSSET & DUNLAP
Published by the Penguin Group
Penguin Group (USA) LLC, 375 Hudson Street, New York, New York 10014, USA

USA | Canada | UK | Ireland | Australia | New Zealand | India | South Africa | China

penguin.com
A Penguin Random House Company

Text copyright © 2014 by Michael Burgan. Illustrations copyright © 2014 by Jerry Hoare. Cover illustration copyright © 2014 by Nancy Harrison. All rights reserved. Published by Grosset & Dunlap, a division of Penguin Young Readers Group, 345 Hudson Street, New York, New York 10014. GROSSET & DUNLAP is a trademark of Penguin Group (USA) LLC. Printed in the USA.

Library of Congress Cataloging-in-Publication Data is available.

ISBN 978-0-448-47945-3   10 9 8 7 6 5 4

Contents

Who Was
Theodore Roosevelt?

On October 14, 1912, a Milwaukee, Wisconsin, crowd eagerly waited to hear Theodore Roosevelt speak. Roosevelt had served as president of the United States several years before, and he was campaigning once again for his old job.

His speech was written on fifty pages of paper that he had folded and stuck in his upper jacket pocket. Outside his hotel, Roosevelt never saw the saloonkeeper who approached him with a gun drawn. Someone in the crowd *did* see the gun and pushed the would-be assassin's arm away, just as the trigger was pulled. The shooter fired once and Roosevelt fell to the ground, but quickly rose. He did not know he had been hit until someone noticed a hole in his overcoat. When he reached inside his coat, he realized he had been wounded. The bulky, folded speech in his pocket, along with the steel case for his glasses, saved his life.

Although he was bleeding, Roosevelt insisted that he give the speech. The crowd could not believe that he would continue to speak rather than go to the hospital after being shot. But Roosevelt told them, "It takes more than that to kill a bull moose."

"Bull Moose" was just one of the nicknames Theodore Roosevelt earned during his long career in politics. Some of the others were Teedie, TR, Teddy (a nickname he hated), and the Trust

Buster. But Bull Moose was a good choice for a man who was physically strong and who was always determined to do things his way.

"I care not what others think of what I do, but I care very much about what I think of what I do! That is character!" he famously said. The Bull Moose was certainly a man of great character.

Chapter 1
New York Boyhood

In 1858, New York City was the largest city in the United States. Almost eight hundred thousand people lived there! Ships arrived at its port carrying a wide variety of goods, including fabric, clothing, and food,

along with people from many countries. Horse-drawn carriages rumbled down crowded streets. And on October 27 of that year, Theodore Roosevelt Jr. was born there.

His father, Theodore Sr., thought the newborn was a pretty baby, but his mother, Martha, nicknamed Mittie, wasn't so sure. She thought her new son looked like a turtle. The Roosevelts already had a daughter named Anna. She and young Theodore were later joined by a little brother, Elliott, and then baby Corinne. For a time Mrs. Roosevelt's sister, Annie Bulloch, also lived with the family.

Teedie, as his parents soon called Theodore, was part of a family that had deep roots in America. The first Roosevelt had come to New York from the Netherlands in 1644. The family bought plate glass in Europe and sold it in America. Teedie's family was quite wealthy. Mr. Roosevelt believed in using his time and his money to help others. One of his concerns was helping orphaned children in New York City to find homes.

ROOSEVELT HOME IN NEW YORK CITY

Young Teedie began his education at home, with his aunt Annie teaching him how to read. For much of his childhood, he battled asthma, which often left him gasping for air and forced him to stay inside. It was during this

ANNIE BULLOCH

time that he discovered his great love of books. As he got older, he became healthy enough to develop his strength and become more athletic.

The Roosevelt children and their parents spent their summers in the country outside of New York City. Oyster Bay, on Long Island, later became the family's second home. In the country, Teedie explored his love of nature and animals.

At nine, he wrote a book describing many of
the insects he had seen. Teedie also sometimes
brought home the animals he studied. It was not
uncommon for snakes and frogs to get loose in

the house. Studying nature—and studying in general—was becoming more difficult for Teedie, because he had poor eyesight. He later wrote that he "had no idea how beautiful the

 world was" until he got glasses at age thirteen. Glasses known as pince-nez, which clipped onto his nose, later became one of his trademarks.

His parents loved to travel and took their children along whenever they could. By the time he was fourteen, Theodore had been to Europe twice and had also sailed down the Nile River in Egypt. Along that famous river, he discovered his love of hunting, which became one of his lifelong passions. During the family's travels, young Theodore also began learning German. Later he would also learn Latin, Greek, and French.

When Theodore turned sixteen, his family decided that he should go to Harvard College.

For a time he thought about studying to become a natural scientist. But after Theodore entered Harvard in 1876, he found himself drawn to history and to public speaking. He would challenge professors in class and argue with fellow students. It was impossible not to notice another of Theodore's well-known features—his large teeth. Cartoonists would later poke fun at him by drawing those choppers even bigger than they were. And once, a newspaper called him "Teethadore."

At Harvard, Theodore gave his first public speech. He sometimes rushed his words, and he spoke with a high-pitched voice that reminded some people of an old woman. But decades later, thousands of people at a time would come out to hear him speak.

Theodore did well at Harvard, and outside of class he enjoyed boxing, riding horses, and rowing.

Theodore suffered a great loss when his father died of cancer in 1878. Writing in his diary, Theodore poured out his sadness. He later told his sister Corinne how important his father had been to him. Throughout his life, before making a major decision, Theodore always considered what his father might have advised.

Theodore finished his studies at Harvard in 1880 and decided to study law at Columbia University in New York. That year, he also married his college sweetheart, Alice Lee. She was a beautiful and charming young woman. Theodore loved her deeply, and he bought her expensive gifts. He promised to spend his money more carefully once he married, but throughout his life he was always generous to his family.

Just before his wedding to Alice, Roosevelt took a hunting trip with his brother, Elliott. They traveled west through Illinois, Iowa, and Minnesota. Theodore battled asthma, a snakebite,

and bitter cold weather. Even so, the trip exploring
the wilderness with Elliott was the first of many.
Theodore loved life on the American frontier.

Chapter 2
First Chances to Serve

Settling down to married life in New York City, Roosevelt began his law studies. He also found a new love: politics. Entering politics, though, was not easy.

Like his father and most wealthy men of the era, Roosevelt was a Republican. He joined the local Republican association, which helped elect party members to government offices. Roosevelt's friends were surprised by this decision. They believed that politics was a career for common men, because politics was a dirty business. Political leaders, sometimes called bosses, could be rough and unpleasant. Roosevelt, however, wanted to be a political leader. He thought wealthy, well-educated men had a duty to enter government and try to make it better for everyone. He was determined to succeed in what he called the "rough and tumble" of New York City politics.

The leaders of the local association liked Roosevelt and helped him win his first political race. In the fall of 1881, he was elected to the New York State Assembly. At twenty-three, Roosevelt was the youngest lawmaker in the house. Alice supported his political career, and Theodore thought having such a charming and pretty wife would help him win political friends.

When he arrived in Albany, the capital of New York State, Roosevelt felt like the new kid in school. He didn't know anyone else and he wasn't sure what to do. But he quickly learned. Other lawmakers got used to hearing his high-pitched voice fill the state Capitol building. He spoke with a distinct accent, turning the word *speaker* into "spee-kar." Roosevelt later became famous for often saying he was "dee-lighted" about

NEW YORK STATE CAPITOL BUILDING IN ALBANY

something. And when he was particularly excited, he described the things he liked as being "bully," meaning "excellent!"

Roosevelt became known as a reformer— someone who wanted to change government and society to help as many people as possible. He supported a law that would improve working conditions for people who made cigars. And Roosevelt believed he had to fight "crookedness" whether it was "great or small."

While serving in the State Assembly, Roosevelt lived only part-time in Albany. On the weekends he headed back to New York City to be with Alice in the new home they had just purchased.

In 1883, the couple learned they were going to have a baby. Roosevelt decided to rent out his new home and have Alice move in with his mother. There, Mittie and Anna could take of her. He began making plans to build a new house in Oyster Bay, near his family's summer home.

ANNA   MITTIE   ALICE

That fall he ran for the Assembly again and
won. In January 1884, Roosevelt returned to
the capital. In New York City, Alice was close
to having her baby. On February 13, while in
Albany, Roosevelt learned he was the father of a
baby girl. But the joy of that news soon soured.
Alice was not doing well, and his mother, Mittie,
had also become very sick. Roosevelt caught a
train home. He found the two most important

women in his life were dying. Both his wife and his mother passed away early on the morning of February 14—Valentine's Day.

The double loss stunned Roosevelt. In his diary that day, he wrote, "The light has gone out of my life." His newborn daughter was named Alice Lee, like her mother. Roosevelt never talked to young Alice about her mother, and he called his daughter by the nickname Baby Lee.

Theodore Roosevelt almost never spoke or wrote about Alice after her death. When he wrote the story of his life in 1913, he didn't mention her once. He had spent years trying to forget his lost love.

Chapter 3
On to Washington

The year Alice died was Roosevelt's last in the
New York Assembly. For most of the summer and
fall of 1884, Roosevelt traveled out west again.
He had bought a cattle ranch in North Dakota
along the Little Missouri River. For a few months
he enjoyed a simpler life. Back in New York City,
his sister Anna took care of young Alice, and work
continued on his new home in Oyster Bay. It
would be called Sagamore Hill.

In the West, Roosevelt often hunted, once spending twenty-four straight hours on horseback. At times he set out alone, cooking the animals he killed over an open fire and sleeping outside under the stars. The vast, open space of the West, he wrote Anna, "has a curious fascination for me."

He soon bought more land and built a new ranch, which he named Elkhorn Ranch. When it was done, Roosevelt filled the wooden home with the trophies of animals he had killed—mounted heads, furs, and skins. Occasionally, he

returned to New York, but he spent much of the next several years in the Badlands of the Dakota Territory. (North and South Dakota were not yet separate states.) The time spent outdoors was good for his health, and when friends back East saw him they marveled at how strong he had become.

As much as he loved the frontier, Roosevelt was still drawn to politics. In 1886 he returned to New York City to run for mayor. He lost the race, but he reconnected with an old friend: Edith Carow.

Roosevelt had known Edith almost his entire life. She and Corinne Roosevelt had been best friends as young children. Edith often spent time at the Roosevelt home and joined them for summers

EDITH CAROW

in Oyster Bay. Theodore sometimes took her out

in a rowboat and had even named the boat for her. On meeting again in the fall of 1885, they began a serious relationship. Soon after, they were married. Edith and Theodore moved to Sagamore Hill with little Alice. They also started their own family. Theodore III, who would be known as Theodore Jr., was born in September 1887.

BENJAMIN
HARRISON

Roosevelt spent much of his time writing the first volumes of a huge history of the American West. Still active in politics, he supported Republican Benjamin Harrison for president in 1888. Harrison won, and he rewarded Roosevelt by offering him a government job. Early the next year Roosevelt went to Washington as a member of the US Civil Service Commission. At first he went alone. Edith was pregnant with their second child, who would be born in the fall. The Roosevelts named him Kermit. Edith, Alice Lee, and baby Kermit joined Roosevelt in Washington at the end of the year. Roosevelt's fourth child, Ethel, was born in 1891.

In his new job, Roosevelt's task was to make
sure qualified people got government jobs, no
matter which political party they supported. In
the past, many of those jobs had gone to unskilled
people, simply because they were friends of
elected officials. As usual, Roosevelt tackled his
new job with tremendous energy. He wanted to
make politicians in both parties follow the rules
for offering jobs. That eagerness upset some

Republicans, who liked being able to reward their friends with government positions.

Overall, Roosevelt loved his job, his family, and his life. He was often heard whistling happily as he walked about. One friend said that for him, "life was the unpacking of an endless Christmas stocking."

Roosevelt was always thinking of his family's future. In 1894, he and Edith had another child, Archibald. He wanted to make sure his children received good educations and enjoyed the easy, comfortable life he had known as a child. He was also thinking about his own future. When he walked past the president's home, then called the Executive Mansion, he imagined himself living there someday. But before seeking such an important office, Roosevelt turned his attention back to New York City.

Early in 1895, he took a job as one of the city's police commissioners. His goal was to end

corruption on the police force. For Roosevelt, that sometimes meant disguising himself and prowling the streets in the early hours of the morning.

One hot summer night, Roosevelt put on a long coat and pulled a hat down over his face. He searched the streets to see if the policemen were doing their jobs. He found one asleep when he should have been on patrol. Another was flirting with a young woman. Roosevelt approached the man and asked, "Is this the way you attend to your duty?" The officer threatened to "fan him" with his nightstick. Roosevelt then informed the

officer who he was and told him to report to his office the next morning.

Roosevelt caught a total of six officers breaking the rules that night. The next morning, he yelled at them about the importance of doing their duty.

He did not punish them, but Roosevelt promised to fine them if he caught them misbehaving again. His efforts to improve the New York police force won him praise from the city's newspapers.

He was winning support among important Republicans, too. In 1896 he strongly backed the party's candidate for president, William McKinley. He traveled across the Midwest giving speeches. If McKinley won the election, Roosevelt hoped to

WILLIAM McKINLEY

work for him in Washington, DC. McKinley did win, and in 1897 he named Roosevelt the assistant secretary of the US Navy. Theodore Roosevelt's political career was on the rise.

Chapter 4
Warrior

In Washington, Roosevelt was eager to make the United States Navy one of the strongest in the world. The country was increasingly exporting goods such as wheat, machinery, and oil to distant lands, like Japan and China. Americans competed with Europeans to buy and sell some of the same items to foreign countries. The European nations

owned colonies around the world, and Roosevelt
thought the United States should own colonies,
too. But having overseas trade and colonies
required a navy to defend American businesses.
And, if necessary, the country had to be ready to
go to war. Roosevelt wanted to build a navy able
to win battles anywhere in the world.

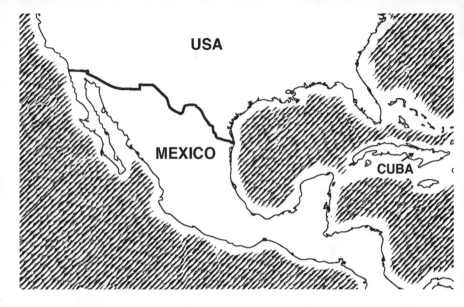

One place that concerned Roosevelt was Cuba.
In 1897, it was a colony of Spain. Many Cubans,
however, wanted their independence, and
for several years they had battled
the Spanish for their freedom.
Americans paid attention to Cuba
because it was so close to Florida
and because its farms produced

two very valuable
crops: sugar

and tobacco. Roosevelt wanted

the US to help Cubans win independence from Spain. Then the United States could play a larger role in the island's economy.

As 1898 began, violence erupted in Cuba. A US battleship, the *Maine*, soon arrived at the island to protect Americans who lived there. In February, the *Maine* mysteriously blew up. Some

Americans blamed Spain. (Historians now know the explosion was an accident.) Roosevelt quickly joined the call for war against the Spanish. He also ordered US naval ships to sail from China to the Philippines, another Spanish colony.

In April, the United States officially declared war against Spain. Theodore Roosevelt wanted to be part of the action. He didn't want to spend the war in an office in Washington. He also knew that success in battle had boosted the political careers of many men before him. Even though he and Edith had just had their fifth and last child, Quentin, Roosevelt made a bold decision. A few months before his fortieth birthday, he quit his job in the Navy Department and volunteered to fight.

Thanks to his adventures in the Badlands, Roosevelt was an excellent shooter and rode horses well. He was given the title of lieutenant colonel and assigned to a cavalry unit. Although technically not the unit commander, Roosevelt

played a major role in finding volunteers. The group came to be called the Rough Riders. At the end of May 1898, about one thousand Rough Riders left their training ground in Texas for Florida, where they waited for orders to sail to Cuba.

When the Rough Riders finally sailed for Cuba, there was room for only 560 of them. Only officers were allowed to bring their horses. Despite the space limits, Roosevelt managed to get two news photographers on board the ship. He wanted to make sure they showed Americans the bravery of his men on the battlefield. He also packed a dozen extra pairs of glasses, in case any were lost or broken. On June 22, the Rough Riders came ashore in Cuba. They were part of a larger US force of about seventeen thousand troops.

For Roosevelt and his men, the deadliest action came on July 1. The Rough Riders were sent to help capture the town of El Caney. Their first target was a building the Spanish held on what the Americans called Kettle Hill. As the battle started, Spanish bullets rained down on the Rough Riders from other hills behind it. Roosevelt rode a horse named Little Texas as his men marched in heat that soared to one hundred degrees.

At the foot of the hill, Roosevelt ordered
aside other troops so his Rough Riders could go
forward. He then led the charge, with a bullet
brushing by his arm. As the Americans went
farther up, Roosevelt got off his horse and led
his men on foot. Soon the Americans controlled
Kettle Hill. From there, the Americans fired on
Spanish troops at nearby San Juan Hill. Roosevelt
then led a second charge up San Juan Hill, and
once again the Spaniards fled.

THE ROUGH RIDERS

WHEN WORD WENT OUT THAT THEODORE ROOSEVELT WAS GOING TO LEAD A CAVALRY UNIT, ABOUT TWENTY-THREE THOUSAND MEN FROM ALL OVER THE COUNTRY VOLUNTEERED TO JOIN HIM. SOME, LIKE ROOSEVELT, CAME FROM WEALTHY FAMILIES IN THE EAST AND HAD GONE TO FINE COLLEGES. OTHERS WERE COWBOYS FROM NEW MEXICO, TEXAS, AND OTHER PARTS OF THE

WEST. SOME WERE NATIVE AMERICANS. A FEW
OF THE MEN WHO DIDN'T KNOW ROOSEVELT
WERE SURPRISED TO SEE HE WORE GLASSES.
"SPECTACLES," AS THEY WERE CALLED, WERE NOT
CONSIDERED MANLY IN THE WEST. TO ROOSEVELT,
THE ROUGH RIDERS WERE "AS FINE NATURAL
FIGHTING MEN AS EVER CARRIED A RIFLE OR
RODE A HORSE."

The war in Cuba lasted several more weeks before the Americans finally won and Cuba was free from Spanish rule. Roosevelt returned to

FOR **GOVERNOR·**

COL·THEODORE ROOSEVELT·

New York in August and found himself a national hero for his bravery in Cuba. The following month he became the Republican candidate for governor of New York. He won the election easily.

Now, at just forty years old, he led the most populous state in the country. Some people referred to him as the "boy governor."

For two years, Governor Roosevelt sometimes battled lawmakers to get the laws he wanted for the state approved. These included a new tax on certain businesses and shorter working hours for women and children. (Children often worked in coal mines and factories at this time.) He became known for the phrase "Speak softly and carry a big stick, and you will go far." Roosevelt meant that you have to back up words with actions. He felt that respect was earned only through hard work and determination. And Roosevelt *was* thinking about going far. He still hoped to one day be president of the United States.

Chapter 5
Path to the White House

As 1900 began, President William McKinley was running for a second term. He was also looking for a new vice president. Republican party leaders chose Roosevelt as McKinley's running mate. The president liked Roosevelt, and the young governor worked hard during the presidential race. Roosevelt traveled the country and spoke in front of several million people. At times, he gave seven or eight speeches each day. In November, McKinley and Roosevelt easily won the election—some people called it a landslide. Roosevelt became vice president in March 1901. He was just forty-one years old.

Roosevelt had few official duties for the first few months. He ended up spending a lot of time

at Sagamore Hill with Edith and the children.
By now, Alice was a young woman of seventeen,
Ted Jr. was almost fourteen, Kermit was eleven,
Ethel was nine, Archie had just turned seven,
and Quentin was a toddler of three. Roosevelt
also took some time to go hunting in Colorado.
Writing back home to Ethel, he said, "I have had
great fun."

Roosevelt was enjoying a leisurely summer. But on September 6, while relaxing in Vermont, he received startling news. President McKinley had been shot by Leon Czolgosz, a former mill worker, while visiting Buffalo, New York. McKinley died on September 14, and Roosevelt was sworn in as the twenty-sixth president of the United States.

At forty-two, he became the youngest president in the history of the country.

To some Roosevelt might have seemed *too* young. But he had almost two decades of political experience behind him and had demonstrated his courage on the battlefield. He had also shown

his great intelligence through the many books he had written over the years. And he could get along with anyone—from the cowboys he met in the American West to the wealthy people he knew in New York.

The American people enjoyed having a youthful

THE TEDDY BEAR

DURING A HUNTING TRIP IN 1902, FRIENDS HUNTING WITH ROOSEVELT IN MISSISSIPPI CAME UPON A SMALL BEAR. THEY CAPTURED IT AND TIED IT TO A TREE SO ROOSEVELT COULD EASILY KILL IT. WHEN THE PRESIDENT SAW THE SMALL, INJURED BEAR, HE REFUSED TO KILL IT. BUT WHEN THE PRESIDENT SAW THAT THE SMALL BEAR WAS SERIOUSLY INJURED, HE ORDERED IT TO BE PUT OUT OF ITS MISERY. WORD OF THIS REACHED THE PRESS. PEOPLE PRAISED HIM FOR SHOWING MERCY ON THE BEAR. A CARTOON APPEARED IN THE NEWSPAPERS OF ROOSEVELT WITH A BEAR CUB AND THE STORY QUICKLY SPREAD. MORE CARTOONS OF THE BEAR FOLLOWED. LATER THAT YEAR, STUFFED BEARS FROM GERMANY WERE BEING SOLD IN NEW YORK AS "TEDDY BEARS." ROOSEVELT WAS QUOTED AS SAYING, "I DON'T THINK MY NAME IS LIKELY TO BE WORTH MUCH IN THE TOY BEAR BUSINESS, BUT YOU ARE WELCOME TO USE IT."

president who seemed to enjoy life and who knew how to communicate openly with them. He often met with the press to discuss the issues of the day. He gave many speeches. Roosevelt called his new office a "bully pulpit," which meant that he was in an excellent position to make his ideas and opinions heard.

Roosevelt was eager to carry out his policies of reform. He wasted no time challenging large companies that were harmful to the country. In 1902 the government started a legal case against a railroad company that Roosevelt thought was too big and powerful. The large company was called a trust. Roosevelt thought the railroad trust should be forced to separate into smaller businesses. After the government won the case, Roosevelt was known as a "trust buster."

Later that year, the country faced a huge coal strike. Coal miners in parts of Pennsylvania refused to work unless they got better pay and

working conditions. The mine owners refused to
meet their demands. Roosevelt stepped in to help
settle the strike. Presidents in the past had usually
sided with business owners when they faced
strikes. Roosevelt said he did not speak for the
owners or the miners. "I speak for . . . the general

public." But he thought the miners should be treated fairly. Roosevelt believed all Americans deserved that fair treatment. It was part of what he called the "Square Deal for the country." The miners agreed to end the strike and accept the proposals of a government commission studying their work conditions. In the end, the miners got their own square deal: more money and a shorter workday.

As president, Roosevelt also focused on international matters. The United States wanted to build a canal in Central America to link the Atlantic and Pacific Oceans. At that time, ships had to sail a long route all the way around the southern tip of South America to go from the East Coast of the US to the West. The

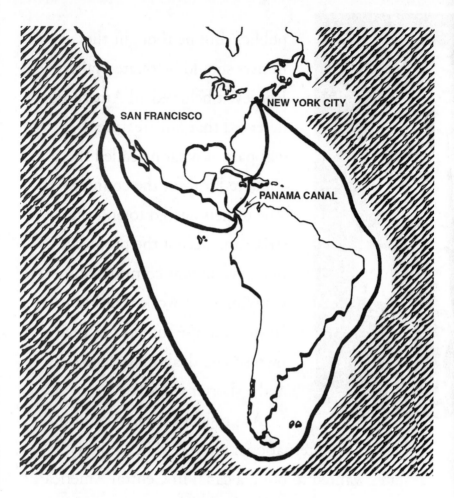

planned canal would shorten the trip by almost
eight thousand miles. Roosevelt mistakenly
thought he had a deal to buy land in what is
now Panama to dig the canal. At that time,

however, the land belonged to Colombia. And the Colombian government was asking for more money than the US wanted to pay.

People in the region of Panama, however, wanted the canal as much as Roosevelt did. So they made plans to break away from Colombia and become an independent country. Roosevelt supported the revolt. In November 1903, he sent warships to the coast of Panama. The rebels in the

region knew the US supported their revolution, and so they arrested their Colombian leaders. The presence of US forces and payments made to Colombian troops ended the revolt peacefully. Panama had its independence, and Roosevelt bought land from Panama for the canal. It wasn't finished until after Roosevelt's presidency had ended. But his actions made the Panama Canal a reality. Three years later, Roosevelt went to Panama. He became the first president to ever visit a foreign country while in office!

THE PANAMA PALINDROME

A PALINDROME IS A WORD OR PHRASE THAT READS THE SAME BOTH BACKWARD AND FORWARD, SUCH AS THE WORD *NOON*. ONE OF THE LONGEST AND MOST FAMOUS PALINDROMES INVOLVES THEODORE ROOSEVELT AND HIS EFFORTS TO BUILD THE PANAMA CANAL: **A MAN, A PLAN, A CANAL: PANAMA!** THE MAN, OF COURSE, IS ROOSEVELT. THE PHRASE WAS CREATED YEARS AFTER ROOSEVELT'S DEATH BY A WELL-KNOWN PALINDROME MAKER, LEIGH MERCER OF GREAT BRITAIN.

Chapter 6
Four More Years

Theodore Roosevelt entered the 1904 race for president with great support from most Americans. They liked his energy and his intelligence, and Roosevelt easily won the election.

In June 1905, he invited diplomats from Japan and Russia to meet with him to discuss a possible peace between the two countries, which were then at war with each other. The diplomats met in

Portsmouth, New Hampshire. There, Roosevelt
and other US officials convinced Russia and Japan
to sign a peace treaty. Roosevelt called the treaty
"a mighty good thing" for everyone. The next

year, he was rewarded for his
work as a peacemaker. He
became the first American
to win the Nobel Peace
Prize. This international

award honors a person or group
that works hard to promote peace in the world.
Woodrow Wilson, Jimmy Carter, and Barack
Obama are the other US presidents who have been
awarded the Nobel Peace Prize since Roosevelt.

Not all of Roosevelt's
time in the White House
was spent on government
affairs. He exercised
two hours a day, playing
tennis, riding horses,
boxing, and even learning
sumo wrestling! An
opponent's punch in one
boxing match caused

Roosevelt to lose sight in his left eye (something few people knew at the time).

He also enjoyed being a father, and his large family filled the White House. Alice always drew plenty of attention. She was the first president's daughter to live in the White House in almost thirty years, and she was sometimes called Princess Alice. She loved fast cars but, of course, back then *fast* meant about thirty miles per hour! She owned a pet snake named Emily Spinach, which she sometimes carried in her purse. Alice also smoked cigarettes in public—which was very unusual for a woman at the time.

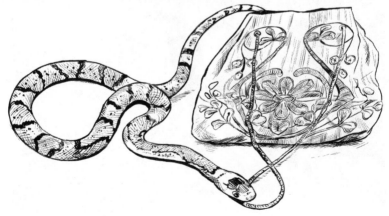

Alice's younger brothers also enjoyed their time in the White House. Quentin established a boys' club in the attic called the White House Gang, and he gave his pet pony a ride in the elevator his father had just installed in the house. During one

of the boys' "battles," Roosevelt rushed out of the house and into the garden, where Quentin had just hacked a garden hose with a fire ax. Roosevelt told his son that it wasn't right to destroy government property. The White House and everything in it belonged to the American people.

Roosevelt had approved changes to renovate and enlarge the White House in 1902 in order to create more office space. In 1906, the "new" White House was the site of Alice's wedding to an Ohio lawmaker, Nicholas Longworth. Details of the wedding filled US newspapers. Before the big day, expensive gifts arrived from world leaders. King Edward VII of England sent a small golden box, while Germany's Kaiser Wilhelm sent diamond

NICHOLAS LONGWORTH

jewelry. All the gifts filled an entire room at the White House and had to be kept under constant guard.

On the wedding day, the bride wore lace that her mother, Alice, had worn when she married Theodore more than twenty years before. When the wedding was over, Edith Roosevelt joked to her stepdaughter, "You have never been anything but trouble." Roosevelt said he could never control his daughter, but he did love her very much.

THE ROOSEVELT FAMILY ZOO

THIS IS JUST A *PARTIAL* LIST OF THE PETS THAT THE ROOSEVELT CHILDREN KEPT WHILE LIVING IN THE WHITE HOUSE:

DOGS	JACK, SAILOR BOY, GEM, SUSAN, RONALD, PINCKNEY, ALLAN, MANCHU, PETE, ROLLO, AND SKIP
CATS	TOM QUARTZ AND SLIPPERS
HORSES	YAGENKA, JOCKO, ROOT, RENOWN, ALGONQUIN, BLEISTEIN, AND WYOMING
HENS	BARON SPECKLE AND FIERCE
RABBIT	PETER
MACAW	ELI YALE
PIG	MAUDE
BEAR	JONATHAN EDWARDS
GUINEA PIGS	ADMIRAL DEWEY, BISHOP DOANE, DR. JOHNSON, FATHER O'GRADY, AND FIGHTING BOB EVANS
BADGER	JOSIAH

President Roosevelt still found the time to travel and hunt. While away, he often wrote letters to his children. He sometimes used family nicknames. Quentin was "Quenty-Quee" and Archie was "Archiekins." In the letters he described things he saw and people he knew. He also often told his children how much he loved and missed them and their mother. The brave hunter and soldier had a soft heart when it came to his family.

Chapter 7
Defender of Nature

Being president brought Theodore Roosevelt
many happy moments. Some of his greatest
successes were on an issue that was close to his
heart—the environment. Years spent in the
country's forests and plains had taught him that
animals and land needed to be protected. Even
though he enjoyed hunting, Roosevelt agreed

with laws that limited where and what a person could hunt and kill. He also knew that those laws were not always enforced. During his travels, he had seen firsthand how the spread of railroads and other businesses threatened the land and the wildlife that lived there.

In 1894, while serving on the Civil Service Commission, Roosevelt had fought to protect Yellowstone National Park in Wyoming. Even though it was already a national park, laws allowed for partial destruction of the Yellowstone land by railroads and mining. He pushed for a new law that would keep businesses and industry out of Yellowstone. Roosevelt also saw the danger of pollution to streams and lakes and the wildlife that lived near them. As governor of New York, he had called for laws to limit pollution in the state.

As president, Roosevelt made protecting the environment of the entire country one of his biggest priorities. He believed in conservation—

saving the country's natural resources: land, air,
water, and wildlife. President Roosevelt helped
create five new national parks and preserve
150 national forests. By setting aside this land
and allowing the federal government to control

it, he ensured that no further development or
destruction could take place there. He also created
national monuments, such as Arizona's Petrified
Forest. He did more than any president before
him to protect the environment.

THE GRAND CANYON

ONE OF THE SITES ROOSEVELT NAMED A NATIONAL MONUMENT DURING HIS PRESIDENCY WAS THE GRAND CANYON IN NORTHERN ARIZONA. IT STRETCHES EIGHTEEN MILES ACROSS AT ITS WIDEST POINT AND IS MORE THAN A MILE DEEP. ROOSEVELT VISITED THE GRAND CANYON IN 1903 AND WAS AWED BY IT. IN A LETTER HOME TO ETHEL, HE CALLED IT "WONDERFUL AND BEAUTIFUL BEYOND DESCRIPTION. I COULD HAVE SAT AND LOOKED AT IT FOR DAYS." TODAY THE GRAND CANYON IS A NATIONAL PARK—AN AREA OF SPECIAL SCENIC, HISTORICAL, OR SCIENTIFIC IMPORTANCE SET ASIDE AND MAINTAINED BY THE NATIONAL GOVERNMENT. MORE THAN FOUR MILLION PEOPLE VISIT IT EACH YEAR.

Roosevelt also wanted trained people taking care of the public lands, to reduce the risk of forest and brush fires. Now called rangers, they also made sure hunters killed no more than the number of birds and animals allowed by law. And when Congress wanted to let business cut more timber in the West, Roosevelt acted quickly. In 1907 he issued an order to protect millions of acres of forests before Congress could pass a law that might have destroyed them.

One of his conservation efforts came at the urging of Frank Chapman, who worked at the American Museum of Natural History. Chapman was the museum's ornithologist—an expert on birds. He knew that Roosevelt had loved and studied birds, since as a teen "Teedie" had donated some of his own birds to the museum. Roosevelt's father, Theodore Sr., had helped create the American Museum of Natural History in New York in 1869.

THE AMERICAN MUSEUM OF NATURAL HISTORY
AS IT LOOKS TODAY

Chapman now hoped that President Roosevelt
would support his idea to create a protected area
for birds, called a sanctuary, off the coast of
Florida. Roosevelt learned there was no law that
stopped him from simply creating the sanctuary
on his own. So, he created Pelican Island National
Wildlife Refuge, the first of fifty-three bird
sanctuaries that he would ultimately create. In

2012 the American Museum of National History honored Theodore Roosevelt's contributions to the conservation effort. It unveiled a new statue of Roosevelt, showing him as he looked on a camping trip to Yellowstone in 1903. He had said that year, "We are not building this country of ours for a day. It is to last through the ages."

Chapter 8
One More Time?

As 1908 began, Roosevelt knew he wouldn't be president for much longer. Since George Washington, no US president had served more than two terms, and Roosevelt did not want to break that tradition. By law, he could have run again, but he said that a "still, small voice" in his head told him it was time to step aside.

Roosevelt supported William Howard Taft for the 1908 election. They were both progressives—people who sought reform. Roosevelt trusted Taft

WILLIAM
HOWARD TAFT

would do a good job. But he also knew he would miss being president. Running the country had given Roosevelt great joy.

Taft did win the election, and Roosevelt left the White House on March 4, 1909. He already had planned a new adventure. He and his son Kermit would soon leave for an African safari. Arriving first in Europe and then Africa, Roosevelt was treated like a hero. Huge crowds cheered him, and he met the leaders of many countries. Reporters wrote about his and Kermit's travels through Africa, where they hunted lions, elephants, and rhinos. Roosevelt also collected plants to bring back to the United States.

Back home, in the fall of 1910, Roosevelt toured the country giving speeches. Huge crowds greeted him. During the trip, he became the first US president to fly in an airplane. (Eight years earlier he had been the first president to ride in a car! He was always up for trying something new.) At an airfield in Missouri, Roosevelt climbed in beside the pilot in the open plane. As the aircraft

flew low to the ground, Roosevelt waved to the people below. Afterward, he called the trip "the finest experience I have ever had."

By 1912, Roosevelt had changed his mind about his old friend Taft. He was not the strong leader Roosevelt had hoped he would be. Roosevelt believed he could improve the country with more progressive ideas—including giving all women the right to vote and creating better conditions for laborers and factory workers—so he decided to challenge Taft for the presidency.

As usual, Roosevelt campaigned hard. He told reporters that he felt as healthy and strong as a "bull moose." His strength, though, couldn't help Roosevelt win the nomination against the sitting president. The Republican Party chose Taft as its candidate for the fall election.

Roosevelt, however, was not ready to give up. He joined with other progressive Republicans to form their own party. It became known as the

Bull Moose Party, with Roosevelt as its candidate for president. The election was a three-way race; Democrat Woodrow Wilson was also running. Roosevelt began to tour the country to seek support. At some stops, he handed out small silver moose charms to the children he met.

For Edith Roosevelt, the campaign was hard. She had hoped several years before that her husband was done with politics. Unlike him, she was a private person and hated the attention the family received from the press. But she knew how much Roosevelt loved speaking in public and campaigning.

On October 14, Roosevelt visited Milwaukee. His speech for that night's talk filled fifty pages of paper, which Roosevelt had folded and stuck in his upper jacket pocket. Outside his hotel, Roosevelt never saw John Schrank approach. Schrank was a mentally unstable man who was determined to stop Roosevelt. He fired one shot

and hit his target. Roosevelt fell to the ground wounded, but he quickly rose. The bulky folded speech in his pocket, along with the case for his glasses, saved his life. Although still bleeding, Roosevelt took the stage, once again impressing Americans with his strength and courage. The audience gasped on learning of the shooting. But Roosevelt assured the crowd that a simple wound couldn't stop a "bull moose."

Back in New York, Edith wept when she heard about the shooting and quickly made plans to go to her husband. Roosevelt rested for several weeks and then began campaigning again. The gunshot wound had won him sympathy—but not enough votes to win the election. Woodrow Wilson was elected president. Roosevelt was disappointed with the loss. He told his son Kermit he wanted to "take as little part as possible in political affairs." But the Bull Moose still had some fight left in him.

DISTANT COUSINS

FRANKLIN DELANO ROOSEVELT

FRANKLIN DELANO ROOSEVELT WAS A DISTANT COUSIN OF THEODORE'S. THEY BECAME CLOSER WHEN FRANKLIN MARRIED THEODORE'S NIECE, ELEANOR. FDR, AS HE WAS LATER CALLED, OFTEN FOLLOWED IN HIS FAMOUS COUSIN'S FOOTSTEPS.

IN 1914, FDR HELD ROOSEVELT'S OLD JOB AS ASSISTANT SECRETARY OF THE NAVY. HE WENT ON TO SERVE AS NEW YORK'S GOVERNOR. AND IN 1932, FRANKLIN ROOSEVELT WAS ELECTED PRESIDENT OF THE UNITED STATES. UNLIKE THEODORE, FDR WAS A DEMOCRAT. BUT LIKE HIS COUSIN, HE TRIED TO USE THE POWER OF THE GOVERNMENT TO HELP AVERAGE AMERICANS. FRANKLIN ONCE CALLED THEODORE "THE GREATEST MAN I EVER KNEW."

ELEANOR ROOSEVELT

Chapter 9
Final Years

At first Theodore Roosevelt did put politics aside. He traveled again within the United States. Then at the end of 1913, Kermit joined him for another grand adventure, a difficult journey to

explore South America. Edith also came for part of the journey. On the trip, Roosevelt visited a region in the Amazon, and a river there was named for him.

Roosevelt returned to New York looking thin and tired. Some people wondered if his days as a public figure were over. But he still loved politics and public battles. He challenged Woodrow Wilson when he disagreed with the president. And one thing they disagreed on was the war that erupted in Europe during the summer of 1914.

On one side, the main countries were France, Russia, and Great Britain. On the other was Germany and Austria-Hungary. Wilson thought the United States should stay neutral and not take sides. Roosevelt accepted this at first, but by 1915 he saw Germany as a great threat to world peace and order. And he thought that Americans should prepare for war.

After German attacks on US ships, the United

States finally did enter the war, in April 1917. Just as he had in 1898, Roosevelt volunteered to lead men into battle. But now, he was almost sixty and at times he suffered from Cuban fever, a disease that first struck him in his Rough Riders days. He

also had high blood pressure. The government denied Roosevelt's request to return to war.

Roosevelt was proud to see his sons Ted, Archie, Kermit, and Quentin join the American forces that went to fight in Europe. Quentin

became a pilot. On one mission, an enemy plane fired at him, killing him just moments before his plane crashed in a field. The news of Quentin's death in July 1918 stunned his parents. It came after Archie had already suffered severe injuries in battle. Edith's heart, Roosevelt wrote, "will ache for Quentin until she dies." Roosevelt said he felt "very bitter" that his smart, talented son had died so young. At Sagamore Hill, the former president was seen with his face against Quentin's horse.

Roosevelt cried as he called out, "Poor Quenty-Quee!"

Despite the great loss, Roosevelt stayed busy. He wrote magazine articles about the war and politics, as he had done for several years. Some people even suggested that he should run as a Republican for president in 1920. But his old energy was gone. His health and the loss of Quentin had taken away much of his strength.

In the fall of 1918, Roosevelt took one last trip out West, visiting several states in support

of Republican politicians. When he got back to New York, he complained of pain in his left leg and feet. His doctors gave him medicine to fight the pain and told him to rest. Around midnight, on the night of January 5, 1919, he laid down on the couch, calling to his valet, "Please put out that light, James." These were the last words the always talkative Theodore Roosevelt ever spoke. Several hours later, he was gone.

Many Americans were shocked to hear that
a man they had always seen as so strong had
died. The Roosevelts held a small ceremony at
Sagamore Hill. Praise for him poured in from
newspapers around the country. Almost everyone
agreed that Roosevelt was a great man who knew
how to have fun and enjoy life. Americans liked
having a leader with those qualities. They also
knew how much he loved the country and wanted

to make it better. His family carried on that tradition, as several of his children became active in politics or the military, and his niece Eleanor, the wife of Franklin Roosevelt, became one of the most famous First Ladies in US history. The Roosevelts were truly a great American family.

Today in South Dakota, a huge likeness of Roosevelt's face, some sixty feet tall, looks out over the Badlands. On his nose sit his familiar spectacles. He is next to three other great presidents, George Washington, Thomas Jefferson, and Abraham Lincoln, in the granite carving on Mount Rushmore. Roosevelt's face was finished in 1939, the last of the four.

To many Americans today, Theodore Roosevelt
may seem like a distant figure. But he worked
hard to serve his country, and he helped shape the
role of the modern president. And he had a grand
time doing it. As he might have said, it was a
"bully" thing to do.

TIMELINE OF
THEODORE ROOSEVELT'S LIFE

1858 — Theodore Roosevelt is born on October 27 in New York City

1880 — He graduates from Harvard with high honors, then marries Alice Lee on October 27

1881 — Roosevelt wins election to the New York State Assembly

1884 — On February 12, Roosevelt's first child, Alice Lee, is born; on February 14, both Roosevelt's wife, Alice, and his mother die

1886 — Roosevelt marries Edith Carow on December 2

1887 — Roosevelt and Edith's first child, Theodore Jr., is born on September 13

1889 — Roosevelt begins working for the US Civil Service Commission; his son Kermit is born on October 10

1891 — The Roosevelts have a daughter, Ethel, on August 13

1894 — Archibald, Roosevelt's third son, is born on April 10

1895 — Roosevelt returns to New York City to serve on the Board of Police Commissioners

1897 — President William McKinley names Roosevelt the assistant secretary of the Navy; on November 19 the Roosevelts' last child, Quentin, is born

1898 — Roosevelt is elected governor of New York

1900 — Running with President William McKinley, Roosevelt is elected vice president

1901 — President McKinley is shot and subsequently dies, and Roosevelt becomes president on September 14

1904 — Roosevelt wins election as president

1918 — Roosevelt's son Quentin is killed while fighting in France

1919 — Theodore Roosevelt dies on January 6 in Oyster Bay, New York

TIMELINE OF
THE WORLD

The Civil War, the battle between Northern and — **1861**
Southern states, begins in South Carolina

President Abraham Lincoln is killed — **1865**

Passage of the Fifteenth Amendment to the Constitution — **1870**
gives African Americans the right to vote

Thomas Edison receives a patent for the lightbulb — **1880**

Mark Twain publishes *Adventures of Huckleberry Finn* — **1884**

German inventor Karl Benz receives a patent — **1886**
for the automobile

X-rays are discovered and soon used in medicine — **1895**

The United States officially takes control of Hawaii — **1898**

Queen Victoria of England dies after leading — **1901**
the country for almost sixty-four years

The Wright brothers fly the first airplane — **1903**

World War I begins — **1914**

A flu epidemic spreads around the world, — **1918**
killing tens of millions of people

World War I ends — **1919**

BIBLIOGRAPHY

Auchincloss, Louis, ed. **Theodore Roosevelt: Letters and Speeches**. New York: Library of America, 2004.

* Brown, Don. **Teedie: The Story of Young Teddy Roosevelt**. Boston: Houghton Mifflin Books for Children, 2009.

* Cooper, Michael L. **Theodore Roosevelt: A Twentieth-Century Life**. New York: Viking, 2009.

* Fitzpatrick, Brad. **Theodore Roosevelt**. New York: Chelsea House, 2011.

Gould, Lewis L. **Theodore Roosevelt**. New York: Oxford University Press, 2012.

* Hillstrom, Kevin. **The Progressive Era**. Farmington Hills, MI: Lucent Books, 2009.

McCullough, David. **Mornings on Horseback: The Story of an Extraordinary Family, a Vanished Way of Life, and the Unique Child Who Became Theodore Roosevelt**. New York: Simon and Schuster Paperbacks, 2001.

Milkis, Sidney M. **Theodore Roosevelt, the Progressive Party, and the Transformation of American Democracy**. Lawrence, KS: University Press of Kansas, 2009.

Morris, Edmund. **Colonel Roosevelt**. New York: Random House, 2010.

Morris, Edmund. **The Rise of Theodore Roosevelt**. New York: The Modern Library, 2001.

Morris, Edmund. **Theodore Rex**. New York: Random House, 2001.

Paterson, Thomas, et al. **American Foreign Relations, Volume 1: A History, to 1920**. 5th edition. Boston: Houghton Mifflin, 2000.

Roosevelt, Theodore. **Autobiography of Theodore Roosevelt**. Blacksburg, VA: Wilder Publications, 2008.

Zacks, Richard. **Island of Vice: Theodore Roosevelt's Quest to Clean Up Sin-Loving New York**. New York: Anchor Books, 2012.

*Books for young readers

WEBSITES

American Presidency Project
http://www.presidency.ucsb.edu/

American President: Theodore Roosevelt
http://millercenter.org/president/roosevelt

Theodore Roosevelt Association
http://www.theodoreroosevelt.org/life/biotr.htm